The People's

Morpeth

by

Evan Martin & George Nairn

Previous page: A Monarch Series postcard of children on the bridge and plodgin' in the river at Stanners.

First published in 2003 by

The People's History Ltd
Suite 1, Byron House
Seaham Grange Business Park
Seaham, Co. Durham
SR7 0PY

ISBN 1 902527 46 1

Contents

Introduction 5

Acknowledgements 6

1. Morpeth Streets Over The Years 7

2. People, Places & Events 45

3. Younger Days 67

4. Old Morpeth Shops & Businesses 79

5. Sporting Morpeth 97

6. Some Nearby Villages 109

Morpeth Olympic Games,

3rd & 5th Augt., 1912.

UNDER NEW MANAGEMENT.

Secretary: Mr. J. Dunn. *Handicapper & Referee:* Mr. Jos. Tully.

Programme for Saturday, 3rd Aug., 1912.

£80 120-yds. Handicap. 1st Prize, £55; 2nd, £10; 3rd, £3; 4th, £2; 5th, £1; 10s. for winners of heats who don't receive money in the final. **(Heats only).**

£15 220-yds Handicap. 1st Prize, £10; 2nd, £3: 3rd, £1; 4th and 5th, 10s. each. **(Start and Finish).**

Pole Leap, £10. 1st Prize, £6; 2nd, £3; 3rd, £1. Medal given if the Professional record is broken.

High Leap, £5. 1st Prize, £3; 2nd, £1 10s.; 3rd, 10s.

Half-mile Foot Handicap, £8 10s.

Half-mile Bicycle Handicap, £7 10s.

10½ Stone Wrestling, £10. 1st Prize, £6; 2nd, £2; 3rd and 4th, £1 each.

12½ Stone Wrestling, £10. 1st Prize, £6; 2nd, £2; 3rd and 4th £1 each.

120-yds. Hurdle Handicap, £6. 1st Prize, £4; 2nd, £1; 3rd and 4th 10s. each.

PROGRAMME FOR BANK HOLIDAY, 5th Augt., 1912:

☞ **Ties and Final of 120-yds. Handicap.**

Local Foot Handicap, 110-yds., £8, for those under 17 and living within a radius of 10 miles of Morpeth. 1st Prize, £5; 2nd £2; 3rd and 4th. 10s. each.

110-yds. Handicap, Start and Finish, £15. 1st Prize, £10 2nd, £3; 3rd, £1; 4th and 5th, 10s. each.

Obstacle Race, £5. 1st Prize, £3; 2nd, £1; 3rd & 4th, 10s. each.

Bolster and Bar, £1 10s. 1st Prize, £1; 2nd and 3rd, 5s. each.

Pony Race (open) 1 mile, under 14 hands, £7 10s. 1st Prize, £5; 2nd, £2; 3rd, 10s.

Quoiting Final, £3. 6 players, 10s. each—£3.

☞ The Programme will be carried out and the above cash prizes given regardless of the weather.

All competitors must appear in proper costume or they will be debarred from competing.

Programme for 1912 Morpeth Olympic Games.

Introduction

As Northumberland's county town, Morpeth has been written about and photographed as much as, if not more than any of the other towns in the county. Certainly, the excellent histories of John Hodgson (1832) and more recently, Harry Rowland, Fred Moffatt, Alex Tweddle and others have benefited those keen enough to furnish their store of historical knowledge.

The written histories of the town tell us of the de Merlays, the de Greystocks, the Dacres, the Carlisles, who in turn 'owned' Morpeth. The thriving cattle markets of the place dominated trade for centuries and the 'murder path' Mor(t) peth town had a thriving community.

With the written histories and the beginning of photography in Victorian times, people could see more clearly what an area was really like. It is further evidence for researchers when town pictures of 100 plus years ago are produced at the flick of a switch.

This book, whilst showing many studies of the streets of Morpeth over the years, also has many photographs of the people of the area. Sporting and recreational groups as well as school classes, many with names, are featured.

It is the authors' aim to help the reader appreciate the past, even if it is only a photograph of Grandma at a VE Day party. There's a bit of nostalgia in all of us.

With luck this collection of over 200 illustrations and a few thousand words of text will please as well as enlighten the wistful amongst us.

Bridge Street in the 1930s looking more like the place we know today. It would be easy to say that it hasn't changed much in seventy years. Certainly the Black Bull Hotel, with its Regency windows, looks familiar and is one of Bridge Street's landmarks.

Acknowledgements

Enthusiastic and knowledgeable helpers are essential in the compilation of a book like this. The authors particularly thank the following for their time and contributions:

Ken Beattie, John Burwood, Mr & Mrs Cassidy, Andrew Clark, Colin Crosby, Keith Creighton, Frank & Elizabeth Dobson, Jack Dunsmore, Marian Easton, Ethel & Jack Elliott, Syd Johnson, Brian Keenleyside, Mike Kirkup, Katrina Mackay, Audrey Miles, Fred Moffatt, Bryan Popely, Jim Robinson, Bill & Eleanor Ricalton, Bernard Scott, Derek Steele, Irene Straughan, Ray Surtees, John Wharrier and Beamish – The North of England Open Air Museum.

Special thanks to Judith Martin for her excellent typing and proof reading.

Kerly Kews – A 1950s photograph taken by Brian Popely. Before the building of the housing estate, this would be a winding path which led to the Victoria Gardens and Price's Tea Rooms.

MORPETH STREETS OVER THE YEARS

Built in 1715 and added to in later years, this was the house of Mr Orde whose House of Correction stood behind here. The property served as a school (upstairs) in the middle of the 19th century but was later bought as a dwelling in 1912 by Mr Robson, the mineral water factory owner. The price of £3,000 was thought enormous at the time. Adams & Gibbons bought Orde House in 1960 and used the buildings for storage. The property was demolished in 1967 and a car showroom and forecourt was later built on the site.

Built in 1714, the architect of the Town Hall was Sir John Vanburgh. Decay caused its rebuilding in 1869-70. The Earl of Carlisle was behind the reconstruction which, although adding to the property was, at the front, stone for stone, a copy of the original.

Recent work on this area has narrowed the roadway in front of the Town Hall. This fine photograph dates from *circa* 1910.

Many regard the Clock Tower as Morpeth's landmark. It has been suggested that the Tower's bells rang for the parish church, but this is hardly true as the old couplet tells you: 'Have you heard of the Morpeth wonder, Church & Steeple a mile asunder.' St Mary's has always had its own bells. The ground floor of the Tower was a short-term prison for offenders and has also housed a pumping station. The clock, which came from Bothal Castle, was unique because for years, it only had one pointer. Another 'hand' was donated by Alderman Cranston, a former mayor, in 1881.

Part of the housing development in the town. Hood Street, *circa* 1905. These brick built dwellings made a huge difference to those described in Morpeth at the beginning of the seventeenth century. Mainly made of timber, they were 'Theked with hedder and straw togedders, or meadow thake and hadder togethers.'

Known for years as 'Singer's Corner' these YMCA buildings, opened in 1905, housed the property from which sewing machine company Singers did a fine trade. In the foreground the Hollon Fountain was originally erected in 1885 by public subscription to remember the generosity of Richard Hollon who, amongst other things, gifted coal to the poor of Morpeth.

Looking down Newgate Street on a sunny day in 1905.

A view from the other side, showing the old Black & Grey Inn, especially popular with the younger element at the beginning of the 21st century. As a contrast, this public house on the corner of Copper Chare and Newgate Street is advertising 'Good Stabling' on its main name board.

The Joiners' Arms, one of Morpeth's favourite watering holes, is at the top of this street (Wansbeck Street). The end of the metal footbridge can be seen. This was built by Swinney of Morpeth and erected in 1869. The bridge lies on the piers of a 13th century bridge, demolished in 1834.

High Stanners as it was a few years before the First World War. This postcard was produced by Graham, Market Place, Morpeth.

The Parish Church of St Mary's. This was built in the 14th century with originally a tower, nave, chancel and a two-storey vestry. In 1830 a small house was erected opposite the porch, as a watchhouse, in which men kept watch for bodysnatchers who, like Burke & Hare, sold newly buried corpses to medical lecturers. At the time it was said £12 was paid for each corpse.

The Court House was built between 1820 and 1828. It was at this time that the County Gaol was built. An octagonal building, it surrounded the Court House but was closed in 1881 and its prisoners transferred to Newcastle. The Court House was the headquarters of the County Constabulary from 1881 to 1939.

Serving King and Country. A parade of soldiers who had accepted 'the King's shilling' lined up in the Market Place, *circa* 1914.

A splendid building, The Playhouse was showing *The Persistent Lovers* when this photograph was taken. One of the two well-patronised theatres in the town. This is now the property of the Iceland company, having been opened as a theatre in 1915.

The Market Place, again on market day. This postcard from Private Allison, No 11 Platoon, Masonic Hall, Morpeth, was sent to his mother in Gateshead.

A photograph from around 1900 showing the corner of Oldgate and Newgate Street before the YMCA buildings were erected in 1905. In front of the Clock Tower is where the butchers stored their tables and equipment from one market day to the next.

The East Mills main building is still standing on the Pegswood Road with the Whorral Bank just off this photograph taken early last century. The mill was rebuilt in 1798, having stood on this site since the beginning of the 17th century.

When it was opened in Howard Terrace in 1905, the Primitive Methodist Church was the latest of the town's churches. It was said to be equipped with modern facilities (schoolroom etc). It was named 'Church' on this photograph but most locals knew it as 'The Chapel'.

Still regarded as one of Morpeth's finest streets, this is Kings Avenue in 1905.

West View. These houses have an excellent view over the Wansbeck. Behind and further down Newgate Street was the old Workhouse which was demolished in 1951, having been built in 1868. The telephone exchange now occupies the site on Newgate Street.

The High Stanners with Abbey Terrace in the background. From a postcard dated 1904.

Above: The Girls' High School established on Newgate Street in 1905, later to become the Girls' Grammar School in 1948. When the three-tier system commenced in 1967, the building became Northumberland Teachers' Centre.

Right: As the Primitive Methodist Chapel, in nearby colliery areas, was known as the workmen's place of worship and often had titles like 'The Pick and Axe Chapel' so the Wesleyans were dubbed members of 'The Pen & Ink Chapel'. The Wesleyans had their Chapel built in Manchester Street in 1884. This is now the Boys' Brigade headquarters.

Above: A view from the Castle showing a prominent Court House and the road leading to Telford Bridge. This photograph dates from *circa* 1925.

Left: In Oldgate stands the Roman Catholic Church; in the gardens of Collingwood House to be precise. The church was dedicated to St Robert of Newminster and was consecrated in 1850.

Right: Post Office staff pictured outside the old post office, *circa* 1905. The entrance is still prominent in the Market Place, being the entrance to the Sanderson Arcade.

This was the time of the 'golden age' of the postcard – many of which make up the illustrations in this book. The picture postcard was licensed by the Post Office on 1st September 1894 and in 1902 the divided back card we recognise today, with both message and address on one side, was allowed. Postcards were used as we use the telephone or e-mail today. You could post a card on the morning and have it delivered that day. Messages such as 'See you this afternoon' are very common on the back of cards. During the period before the First World War there could be three or four deliveries a day in some areas.

Below: Morpeth post ladies and one postman ready for deliveries. How many postcards are they delivering?

St Robert's Presbytery in 1912.

The Catholic Church from a different angle, *circa* 1902.

Newminster Abbey was founded by Randolph de Merlay, the second Baron of Morpeth. In 1138, eight monks took possession of the new Abbey which was, in structure, very much like Fountains Abbey, near Ripon. It was the home of Cistercian monks, but fell foul of Henry VIII's dissolution policy of the 16th century.

The beautiful interior of St James' Church, which was consecrated in 1846. The silver vessels and candlesticks used in the consecration were stolen from the church within a week and were never seen again.

Above: At the end of Lady's Walk is Springhill. This is on the hill on the road to Mitford above Newminster Abbey. Sir George Renwick MP lived here.

Left: Sir George Renwick – Publicity leaflet for the 1922 General Election.

Standing in a prominent place at the end of Telford Bridge and Bridge Street is St George's United Reformed Church. Built in 1860 it stands on the site of a millrace.

This visit, at the beginning of last century, by General Booth of the Salvation Army, commanded a large attendance in Castle Square.

The original Elliott Bridge was erected in 1925 and rebuilt in 1982 with a taller structure. Carlisle Park, in the foreground, was a gift to Morpeth, in 1915, from Lady Carlisle. Pretoria Avenue is in the background, built in 1900 at the time of the Boer War.

The Elliott Bridge being launched over the Wansbeck in 1925. The Town Hall roof can be seen to the left of the picture.

Two views of East Cottingwood in the grounds of St George's Hospital.
In 1745 General Wade's army marched north to try to suppress the Jacobites under Bonny Prince Charlie. He camped at Cottingwood and Morpeth's bailiffs had to help the General as much as possible. This entailed carting baggage with labourers clearing hedges to improve the roadway north. The improvement to the roads was highlighted in the verse:

'If you had seen these roads before they were made,
You would lift up your hands and bless General Wade.'

The Cenotaph with the Castle ruins and Gatehouse in the background in 1925. William de Merley, Morpeth's first baron, commissioned the Castle building which was completed in 1129. The Gatehouse was completed in the 14th century.

The Chantry building in peaceful surroundings with Fail's shop, Thew's café and bakery prominent.

As its name suggests, Oldgate is the town's oldest street. Taken from the back of the Tower, it is quiet enough for swans to walk along.

A view of Morpeth around one hundred years ago. This photograph was taken from the south.

Lots of changes have been made to the Baysland area since this old panoramic view was taken.

The 1930s and the United Bus Company finds a useful 'station' in front of the Town Hall.

The grand ivy clad houses of River View, *circa* 1910.

A good panoramic study of the river and town from what is now the Elliott Bridge area. This postcard photograph is postmarked 1905.

A mixture of carts, motor bikes and motor cars in Bridge Street in the mid 1920s. The pillion passenger on the motor bike and side car is riding side saddle! Jennings Garage is on the right.

The Castle grounds from a picture postcard dated March 1930.

This photograph of around 1910 shows what a variety of shapes, sizes and designs of buildings make up Newgate Street.

Bicycle riding wouldn't be pleasant in 1905, if this example of roads is anything to go by. Station Road, here pictured, would be dubbed 'clarty' by the locals.

About 100 years ago and what could be a quiet Sunday morning on Bridge Street.

Bridge Street, not so quiet, on a market day in 1905.

A photograph, taken in 1931, from the Telford Bridge looking onto Castle Square.

Turn the clock back a few years, and the camera around, and this is the view of the old tollhouse and Telford Bridge. The tollhouse was in later times a sweet shop. One of the last shopowners was Mrs Ashby who worked for many years in Bertha Burns teashop.

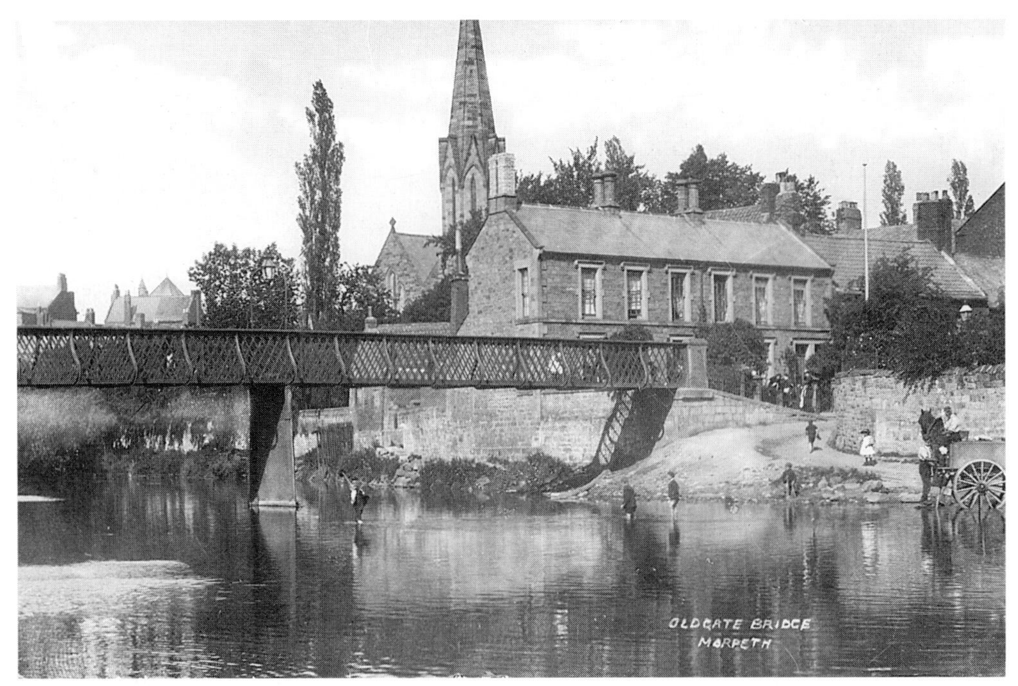

One of the four bridges to cross the Wansbeck at Oldgate since 1830. This particular bridge was moved to Gas House Lane in the early 1930s.

A busy photograph of Newgate Street around 1910, with Charles Harrison's popular jewellers shop at No 1 Market Place. Alfred Tyler's boot & shoe shop at No 12 Newgate Street can be seen on the right, with Mrs Elizabeth Noble's hardware shop opposite.

The talking point on a Fair Day, nearly one hundred years ago, was Walter Murphy's amusements. Every year he apparently had something different. This Venetian Gondola ride held pride of place in the centre of the town. Fairs were regular events at Whit and in September.

With St Robert's Church, Mattheson's Gardens and the Workhouse as a background, this is where Romanys had one of their small camps, over many years. Their particular language is still used by many Mopethians (gadgies). 'Deek', 'Mort', 'Jugal' and 'Mar' are words amongst others bandied about.

This postcard dated 1905 shows the exterior of Morpeth Station. The NER horse and cart to the right of the picture would be a common sight around the town and surrounding villages, picking up and delivering parcels. The main East Coast Railway Line through Morpeth opened in 1847 with the Blyth and Tyne branch using the main station in May 1880.

This 1905 postcard of Morpeth Station was sent to Jane Cassidy who at the time was working for Finlay's Tobacco Stall on North Shields Station. The W.H. Smith bookstall can be seen on the right of the picture. The adverts are for a week on the Rhine or a week in Lucerne for £5.

Above: T.H. Finlay Tobacconists on Morpeth Station with Miss Jane Cassidy behind the stall. Finlay's were a well known tobacconists in the North East with outlets in various parts of Newcastle, No 1 Bridge Street, Morpeth, and railway stations at Hexham, North Shields, Tynemouth and Whitley Bay.

Right: Miss Jane Cassidy poses outside T.H. Finlay Tobacconists kiosk on Morpeth Station, circa 1904. Jane also worked for Finlay's at North Shields Station and lived in Newgate Street, Morpeth. She sold 'El Dronte' cigars at 3d each or five for one shilling.

The High Church area is hardly recognisable today from this study of the Sun Inn and surrounding properties of bygone years. The Sun was the first clubhouse of Morpeth Golf Club.

Lucas of Newcastle's 'digger' ploughs up the road in Newgate Street, helping to fix a burst water main. The Old Fire Station has long gone and this is now an entrance into Dawson Place.

The Hollon Fountain, erected in 1885, was demolished in an accident in 2001 but was restored in 2003. This Grade II listed monument is in most photographs of Morpeth Market Place and this small selection from early days to more modern times shows the fountain could tell a few stories.

Probably the oldest photograph of the fountain. The buildings behind are unrecognisable today as the corner of Oldgate and Newgate Street.

The fountain's lamp is just visible in this late Victorian picture of market day hustle and bustle.

Edwardian times with the cattle and folk mingling.

No cattle, but plenty of shoppers and a muddy road to contend with.

A few years later and the road is being covered with pebble stones.

The 1920s it seems by the dress and vehicles.

More up-to-date times and the Hollon Fountain with a different lamp and signs for motorists attached. A 'quiet' picture from 1955.

PEOPLE, PLACES & EVENTS

Mayor's Sunday is still held annually. The idea is for the Mayor to give a treat to his fellow councillors. This top hatted gathering was Mayor Dowie's day on 12th November 1933. The familiar face on the far right is that of Alfred Appleby.

Miss Emily Wilding Davision died from injuries she sustained when she went under the King's racehorse 'Amner'. The incident was captured on camera by the famous photographer Francis Frith at the 1913 Epsom Derby. She lay in a coma for four days and died on 8th June. Emily's funeral was one of the largest at the time seen in London. The coffin was transported from King's Cross to Morpeth Station and this Graham Series postcard of Morpeth shows the cortege from Morpeth Station to St Mary's Church where the recently refurbished monument can be seen in the churchyard.

Swinneys girls, during the First World War period, making shells. The man with the pipe is Bart Ridley.

A regular sight in Morpeth in June was the Northumberland Miners' Picnic. Always attended by huge crowds, this 1920 gala was no exception.

Bands were always popular in the area with playing at the Miners' Gala an annual event. This is the Northumberland Hussars new band pictured in November 1936.

Young soldiers to be, at King Edward's. The army cadet troop was partly led by Morgan (Monty) Williams, a Welsh teacher at the school. He is the larger man in the middle of the front row.

More grown up soldiers were the Home Guard. This photograph of 1944 shows Major Rutherford of Rutherford's shop in the Mr Mainwaring part. Among his troops are: Mick Appleby, Paddy Cordray, John Munday, George Moor, Jimmy Robson, Ray Newman, Tommy Appleby, Tom Thompson, Edwin Moor and Jim Fogarty.

Celebrating the fact that war was over, at least in Europe, are the folk of West Greens in 1945.

A few months later and victory over Japan (VJ Day) was glorified with a party by the West Greens folk in Goose Hill School.

Not to be outdone, Morpethians from the other end of town (Buller's Green) have their VE Day party too.

Yet another VE party. This one is at Granby Buildings and included in the picture are: Mrs M. Popely, Mrs Allison, Mrs Daglish, Mrs Waldie, Mrs Brooks, Mrs Lamb, Miss Waldie and Miss Maclean. The children include: Frank Waldie, Walter Allison, Billy Allison, Bryan Popely, Pat Popely, George Popely, Ann Brooks, Billy Brooks and Noel Lamb.

Still celebrating, but 32 years later, this street party was to celebrate HM the Queen's 25 years on the throne. The place is Alexander Road, Middle Greens.

The Econofreeze shop in Newgate Street was at one time a branch of the Co-op. Back row: Audrey Wilson, Molly Twist. Middle: Violet Redpath, Miss Goldsberry (manageress), Betty Craigs. Front: Lillian Gordon and Eleanor Smith. These were the staff members in 1952.

The staff of R. Elliott's haulage business on an outing to Bridlington, *circa* 1938. The trip was paid for by the company and was looked upon as their annual holiday. Back, left to right: Fred Cooper, Bob Riddle, Billy Riddle, George Manley, Bob Durey, Bob Appleby, Bob Storey, M. Huntley, Fred Hopper, Joe Williamson and Bob Manley. Front: Jimmy Smith, Heck Smith, Jim Smith, Mr Straughan, Dave Givens, L. Davison, Tom Riddle, Roger Barnston, Matty Sanderson, Alan Creighton, Tot McLevy, Johnny Pringle, George Banford, Jos Nichol and Jack Elliott.

Back at work and posing in the New Market with Elliott's vehicles are: Arthur Dodds (FJR160), Heck Smith (FNL304), Joe Wilkinson (FNL253) and Bobby Riddell (EJR338).

The Woolworth's staff of 1941. All have smiles for the camera. The ladies in white in the back row are: L. Saint, C. Hunter and M. Hare. The front row includes: M. Smith, Nancy Brewis, H. Dunn, Miss Chard (manageress), T. Smith, J. Baird and J. Fairbairn.

Waiting to start the soup course at their annual dinner are members of the United Bus Company. Included are: the three Pringle Sisters, Larry Sheerin, Allen Ricalton, George Bewick, Gladys Bewick, Alf Scott and Winnie Pickering. Date unknown.

A super night out was to be had by the staff of Rutherford's and their partners. Also present were workers from Smail and Armstrong & Angus. This was an annual event held in the Parochial Hall (later YMCA Hall). This particular get-together was in 1934.

The Clock Tower restoration appeal brought out the Mayor, Bert Jobson, and his wife Cilla at the carnival in 1950.

Going back to 1907 and the Rechabites in Morpeth were governed by this board of moustached and bearded directors.

Thursday, 7th March 1963 caused all sorts of problems for pedestrians and drivers.

Wellies were an absolute necessity and the flooding was as bad as anyone could remember.

All hands to the pumps as a petrol tanker caught fire on Newgate Street, with exploding petrol cans shooting all over the street. The date was 4th January 1923 and the location was outside Albert Penn's boot repair shop at No 42. But the biggest problem was Mr Penn's fish and chip shop over the road at No 43.

The sort of shop front no owner wants to see. This 1950s fire was at Jobson the Saddler's overlooking the market.

Edwardian times and a particularly cold winter, *circa* 1910. This gave the youngsters, and some older skaters, the opportunity to use the Wansbeck as an ice rink. This photograph fronts a postcard and the correspondent has written on the back, 'The ice was bearing hundreds of young people who found leisure time to go and slide up and down regardless of the danger and the biting cold.'

The Wansbeck, when the ice has broken up.

The annual Morpeth Gathering, usually running for three days in the spring, began in 1966 as a modest concert of Northumbrian music and song. It is now one of the prestigious events in the Northumbrian calendar. The proceedings begin with the entry into the town of the Border Cavalcade, a re-enactment of the return of Lord Greystoke from the Battle of Otterburn in 1388. The parade is headed by two pipers, dressed in traditional costumes, to be welcomed by the Morpeth Gadgy (*right*).

One of the main instigators of the Gathering in modern times was the late Roland Bibby who did so much to keep alive the Northumbrian dialect and way of life. His daughter Kim Bibby-Wilson is now at the helm.

The Gathering is packed with traditional crafts, music, song and poetry when local artisans, composers and writers can join together in producing all that is good, Northumbrian style.

The final event, normally held in the Town Hall, features the previous year's winning entrants in the song-writing and verse speaking contests, providing a concert which always plays to a packed, appreciative audience. Fifty editions of a magazine named *Northumbriana*, a great legacy compiled by Roland Bibby, containing articles, poems and stories, musical compositions, tunes and songs, is living proof that the Northumbrian culture is very much alive.

Pipers lead the parade for the Gathering.

Roland Bibby.

Right: Amateur dramatics are forever popular. The YMCA drama group, including one or two teachers, performed at their centre in Dark Lane.

MORPETH Y.M.C.A. DRAMA GROUP

PRESENTS

"BLACK TULIP"

A THRILLER BY SAM BATE

CAST:- JEANNE TODD, ANNE FORSTER, RALPH MAUGHAN, CORDON BOOKER, KEITH SWAILES, JIM PERRIS, ANNE COCKBURN, HAZEL DENT, BARBARA PILE

Y.M.C.A. Centre, Dark Lane, Morpeth

Thursday, Friday & Saturday 14th, 15th & 16th, MAY, 1970 at 7-30 p.m.

BOOKING OFFICE Y.M.C.A. (Tel. 2332)

Admission by Programme 3s.6d. O.A.P.'s & Children 2s.

MAY 4TH

Below: Mitford Road School in 1949 and *The Bishop's Candlesticks* was the play. Among those in the action: B. Jones, A. Milner, L. Smith, H. Simpson and B. Caisley.

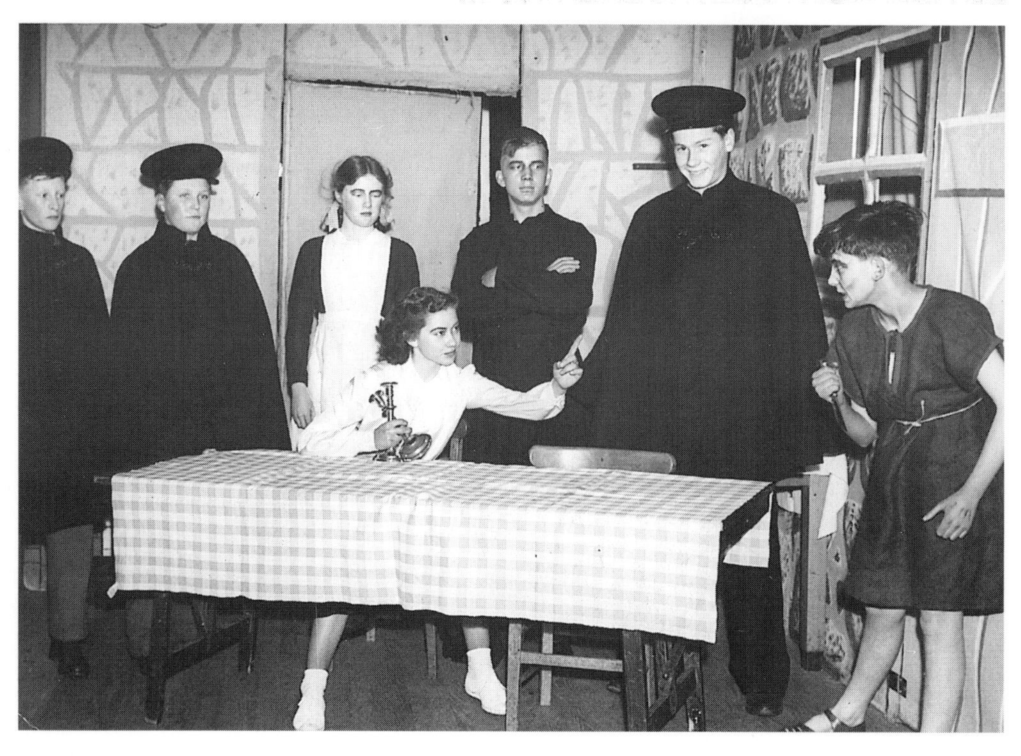

The colourful Brough's vans were easily seen around the area. This is the Morpeth version with Mattie Parkin its driver. Brough's shop was on Bridge Street.

The Rectory Garden Party, *circa* 1955. In charge of this stall is Miss Dodds, on the far right. On her right is Miss Douglas, who was Dr Stenhouse's receptionist for many years.

There were many floats at the Coronation parade. This 'Sporting Float' had L. Heslop (golfer), J. Young (tennis), T. Horne (rower), S. Ratcliffe (weightlifter), L. Smith (runner) and others.

Rotaract, a junior form of Rotary, was formed in the town in the 1970s. Keith Creighton, pictured here at an art exhibition, was its first president. With Keith are: Julie Stephenson, Delphine Blenkinsopp and June Landles.

Morpeth Camera Club Exhibition, 1957. Left to right: A.E. Naylor, John Wallace, Councillor Bert Jobson, Lord Romney (National President YMCA), Councillor Alf Appleby (Mayor of Morpeth) and Colonel E. Graham Angus (President NE Division YMCA).

Mr John Wallace and members of the Morpeth YMCA knitting club.

From a postcard dated February 1916, the High Stanners swing park is very popular.

From the 1950s, this travelling fair has an equally busy time.

A meeting of the Hunt outside the Newcastle House Hotel. Master of the Hounds was Eric Steel who lived in Newminster House. Behind him is Jack Hine from Longhirst Dairy. The man walking in the foreground is Dick Elliott. The date is somewhere in the late 1940s

Morpeth was visited by King Edward VII in 1905 and his grandson, the Prince of Wales, is seen outside the Town Hall on his visit in 1923. Fourth from right (standing) is W.S. Sanderson who, in later years, was known as 'Mr Morpeth'.

One of the oldest buildings in the area, West High House farm. Restoration can be seen on the right, with the original stone blocks at the base; the rest made up of bricks.

One of Morpeth's characters, Joe Cook, manager of the Nag's Head, before the Second World War. He's pictured here in 1936 with Eleanor Smith (now Ricalton).

YOUNGER DAYS

Morpeth 5th Boy Scouts in 1944.

The Primrose family of Morpeth were very well known photographers. Schools in the area regularly had them for class and individual photographs. Not all these groups were photographed by Primrose but many were.

A *circa* 1920 photograph of St James' School. Mr Raitt was the teacher.

An early Second World War photograph of St James' School. The building was on the site of the car park behind the Boys' Brigade hall in Manchester Street. Miss Carr was the headmistress at the time, supported by Miss Jury and Miss Grant. Amongst the children are: Tommy Mather, Tom Popely, Les Brown, William Angus, A. Allan, Sheila Stockdale, George Brown, Green, Ruth Pickard, Jean Patterson, Alice Patterson, G. Kay, Peggy Wallace, Elsie Mowitt, Hedley, Ron Familton, Harry Cooper, J. Bolton, Anne Scott, Hedley, John Angus, Dorothy Moffat, Dick Swindle, Norman Mather, Sheila Pochon, Betty Brown.

Mr Garbutt was headteacher at Morpeth Secondary Modern School in 1949. This class 2A, with Mr Grocott as its teacher, includes in the back row: A. Gibson, J. Gibb, E. Allen, L. Smith, H. Simpson, B. Partington, B. Alder, G. Brown, B. Jones, G. Robertson, I. Scott. Centre row: L. Nicholson, H. Black, A. Varvill, M. Tweedy, A. Martin, A. Milner, S. Icerr, J. Mallory, V. Henry, M. Wilson, L. Forster, C. Wilson. Front Row: J. Stevens, H. Brown, E. Pratt, S. Hills, V. Williams, Mr Grocott, L. Robson, J. Patterson, B. Pearson, unknown, S. Mitcheson. Sitting: A. Tweddle, B. Hetherington, P. Kelly and D. Scrowther.

The year was 1949 and the class 4A at Morpeth Secondary Modern. Pupils are listed as, back row: Jimmy Renton, Harold Henderson, Keith Allon, Robin Wilson, Billy Ricalton, David Pantry, John Warwick, George Reynolds, Noel Lamb. Middle row: Dennis Coulson, Jack Common, Lionel Turnbull, Ian Clark, Margaret Lawson, Ann Pearson, Derek Hall, Brian Reid, John Wood, Frank Creighton. Front row: Sheila Grix, Gwen Rutherford, Mary Routledge, Norma Marley, Celia Cummings, Mr Bowman, Eleanor Smith, Audrey Potter, Isobel Nixon, Pauline Stephenson and Mona Tipper. Missing from the photograph: John Gibson, Evelyn Whellan and Nora John.

A carefully posed postcard of King Edward VI Grammar School. Note the boys under the tree and at the top of the steps.

Another early postcard of the Grammar School taken from a similar angle. This time the boys are playing cricket. The school has always been well known for its sporting feats, especially in rugby and cricket. Well coached cricketers of a high standard were synonymous with Morpeth Grammar School.

Morpeth Grammar School on its foundation charter of 12th March 1552, was named 'The Free Grammar School of King Edward the Sixth' for boys and young men to be instructed in grammar by one master and one under master. The original school buildings were the Chantries. The more recognisable building here, had its foundation stone laid in 1858, it being added to over succeeding years.

Morpeth Grammar School prefects, 1953. Back row: Peter Fowler, Michael Crow, Derek Steele, Terrence Mitchell, Cedric Wilkinson, John Tait, John Mabon. Front row: Harry Sewell, Donald Irvine, Jimmy Turnbull, Mr E. Anderson, Mr G. Howell (headmaster), Mr Willaims, unknown, Ron Jackson and Stuart Miles.

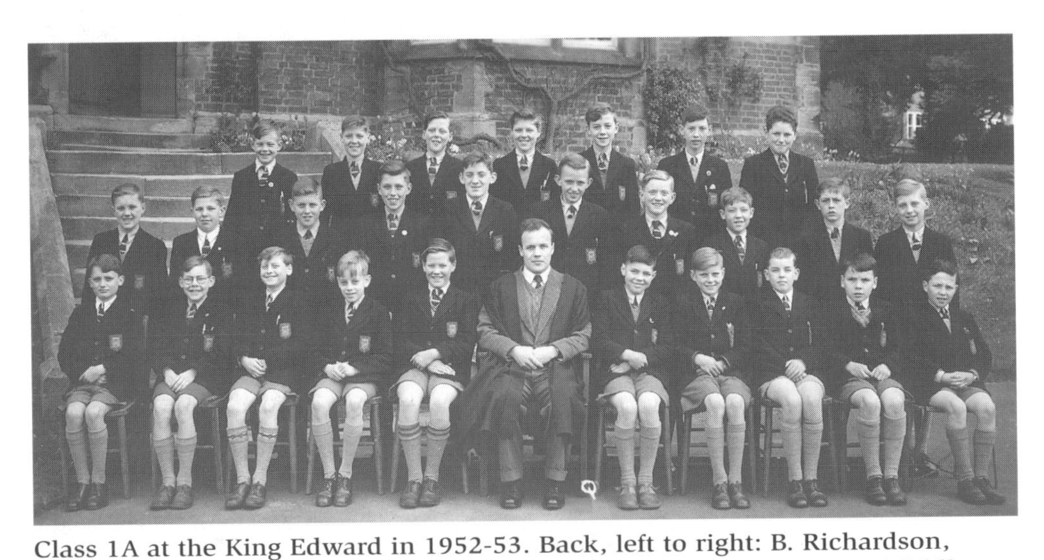

Class 1A at the King Edward in 1952-53. Back, left to right: B. Richardson, N. Orkney, ? Owen, K. Orkney, D. McCowey, R. Henderson, B. Scott. Middle: A. Dent, T. Kelly, B. Main, H. Little, W. Bates, W. Jacques, A. Summers, H. Angus, R. Thompson, R. Miller. Front: W. Mountain, A. Cutter, ? Crave, R. Tyson, R. Bolton, Mr Colin Danskin, D. Simpson, ? Sparrow, H. Smith, D. Humfries and D. Smith.

These three photographs were taken at a reunion for former pupils from the King Edward VI Grammar School. The reunion took place at the White Swan, Morpeth, July 2002.

Above: Bill Henderson, Harry Dobson, Frank Ward, Bill Hindmarsh and Michael Singer.

Right: Ian Turnbull and Alan Daglish.

Below: Gordon Mordue, Stuart Miles and Mike Smith.

A group taken in 1950 of pupils from the Girls' Grammar School. Miss Gendall was the headteacher. Names of the girls are not available.

For many years Miss Gendall was headteacher of the Girls' Grammar School. She is pictured here in July 1959 with some of her senior girls. The girls include: Linda Hogg, Maureen Primrose, L. Henderson, Euna Skilling, Margaret Tilley, Lorna Dixon, ? Dickinson, Margaret Purvis, Eileen Main and Hazel Chandler.

Morpeth Girls Grammar School, 1948. Back row: Eileen Baker, Brenda Brown, Cathy Reid, Anne Barker, Dylis Johnson, Ena Noble, Winifred Conn, Freda Robson, Elsie Thompson, Jeanne Graham, Brenda Arkle, Jean Thompson, Ellen Brown, Mavis Tapley. Middle row: Audrey Cookson, Greta Young, Norma Tyson, Mary Robson, Rita Bradshaw, Helen Pringle, Marion Lyall, Jean Pearson, Janette Hay, Jane Heaslet, Eva Rees. Front row: Eleanor Robertson, Shirley Rutter, May Hine, Jean Graham, Dorothy Wardhaugh and Pat Graham.

Over 50 years later many of the girls met for a reunion at Morpeth Golf Club. Back row: Jean Pearson, Mary Carmichael, Marion Lyall, Mary Robson, Rita Bradshaw, Anne Barker. Middle row: Pat Graham, Shirley Rutter, Audrey Cookson, Joyce Appleby, Grace Stephenson, Janette Hay, Norma Tyson, Ena Noble. Front row: Sheila Batey, Jeanne Graham, June Elliott, Dorothy Wardhaugh, Brenda Arkle, Jean Jacques, Nancy Brown and Elsie Thompson.

Newminster Modern School netball team 1959.

The official staff photograph of Newminster Secondary Modern School in 1959 included, back: John Wharrier, Bill Brown, Peter Thompson, Tom Adams, John Towers, Graham Williams, Tom Williams, John Haddon, Ben Skilling. Included front: Miss Tarber, Dorothy Batey, Miss Joisce, Pat Orange, Katy Douglas. Seated: Wilf Stoker.

The Queen's Coronation in 1953 was a great time for celebration, especially for youngsters. These two photographs show the YMCA display – on the back of an Elliott lorry – for the Coronation Parade.

The first Morpeth Company of the Boys' Brigade, *circa* 1950. Taken at Parochial Hall, Morpeth. Now the site of Admiral Collingwood Court. Among those included: John Parkin, Ron Gibb, Neville Croudace, George Richardson, George Lee, Allan Daglish, John Robson (Flag), Norman Martin, George Thompson, George Popely, Gilbert Robertson, Joe Gibb, Bob Noble, Walker, C. Darroch, Peter Kelly, George Short, Malcolm Fairbairn, Bill Leatham, Donnie Common, Donnie Carmen, Billy Caisley, Billy Stanners, Bryan Popely, Dennis Moore (Officer), Ken Chirnside (Officer), Thompson Caisley (Officer), Alderman R. Elliott (haulage contractor and Boys' Brigade sponsor), Captain R. Lumley, Mr Lumley, Tim Stanners, Peter Trotter, Howard Swanson, John Mason, T. Caisley, Billie Harvey, Peter Appleby, John Snarr, Les Cregcian and Harry Daglish.

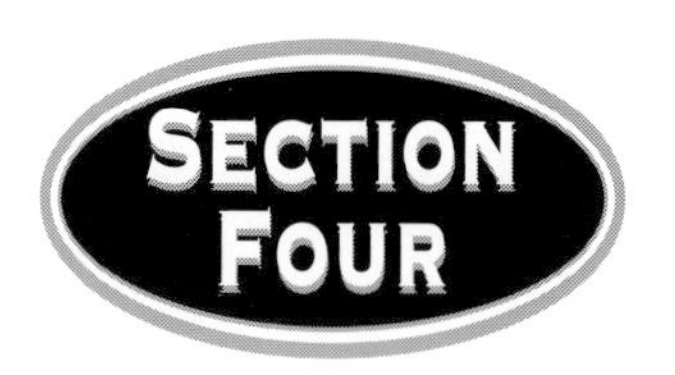

OLD MORPETH SHOPS & BUSINESSES

Proctor's Cabinet and Furniture Showrooms at No 35 Newgate Street with a patriotic display of flags above the door. It has been suggested that this was to celebrate the end of the Boer War. It's more likely to be the end of the First World War, judging by the countries represented. This property is now Proudlock's House and Home shop.

Bridge Street

Left: G. Rutherford & Co, established in 1846, is obviously one of the oldest businesses in the County. Their advertising in 1907 suggested it was the best place in the district for drapery, medium and good class. This is the property of No 10 and they also had a 'ladies' underclothing shop' at No 36.

Below: Mackay's Herald Office at No 19 has barely changed its frontage in almost 100 years. This is a lovely shop front, full of character. In a prime position, it enhances the old fashioned feeling that a walk around the town can give you.

Dance & Carr: Pastry Cooks and Caterers had premises at No 13 and a restaurant in the YMCA buildings on Market Place.

The Oxfam shop now occupies No 27, Bridge Street but established in 1880 and occupying these premises was John Bowman Garvies, Saddlers. He was also a harness maker and ironmonger and had only been in these premises for a few months when this photograph was taken in 1907.

'Market for Menswear, Centre for Clothing & Headquarters for Hats' so went the advertisement for E.D. Soulsby's menswear establishment at No 29 Bridge Street. It further stated 'Our desirable goods and low prices are bound to bring customers.' The building, in 2003, is occupied by Northern Rock.

Above: At No 30 was James Whittle, Chemist and Druggist who was fully qualified by exam, as his advert informed. Whittle also sold sheep dips and cattle medicines. This is now the Cancer Research charity shop.

Left: Vying for business with Soulsby's was the hosiers and drapers Armstrong & Angus and they were at No 31. They sold all sorts of gents' and ladies' clothing and were agents for Aertex cellular clothing, popular at the time. This is now Superdrug.

The Home and Colonial stores were to be found at No 32 Bridge Street. Bargain of the day was a tuppence dividend for every shilling spent on 'Perfect' brand margarine.

A bigger premises at No 38 was George B. Grey who sold all kinds of clothing. He also had a furnishing department. Barclay's Bank now use No 38.

Newgate Street

No 17 belonged to R. Oliver & Sons, flour millers and commercial merchants. A large bakery also produced all manner of bread and pastries, including muffins and crumpets. Now the offices of News Post Leader.

Hermann Pluss-Hill had a large family premises as he could cater for 100 guests at any one time. He was a caterer and confectioner. His advertisement told everyone his restaurant was a cyclists' rest with special accommodation for clubs.

Above: The advert to attract people here stated: 'The best and most reliable house in the town for notepaper, envelopes, sundry stationery, books, periodicals and magazines.' Fountain pens were on sale from 6½d to 17/6d each. J.J. James was here at No 8 for many years. Callers Pegasus now occupy the site.

Right: Any decorating to be done and you could find Robert Jackson, decorator, in 'The White Shop' at No 28, Newgate Street. Simply Silver is the occupant now.

Left: 'We keep a large stock of churns, butter workers and all dairy utensils and general and furnishing ironmongery.' So declared Pentland & Company at No 34 Newgate Street. Judging by the outside shop display, a steel helmet worn on entry would be a good idea. F.H. Hardy the florists now occupy the site.

Below: The fact that Morpeth was a self-contained community, which catered for the public's every need is emphasised by this photograph. The owner of the shop on the right was Francis William Rowe of No 64 Newgate Street and it is probably just as well there isn't a full frontal of his shop window. His trade in Kelly's Directory of 1924 is described as 'Tripe Dresser'.

Above: No 60 Newgate Street and the corner of Manchester Street was James Elliott's strange mixture of fruit, flowers and stationery. As this photograph shows, the window displays are very tidy and would encourage customers. The premises are well known in the town now as Appleby's Bookshop.

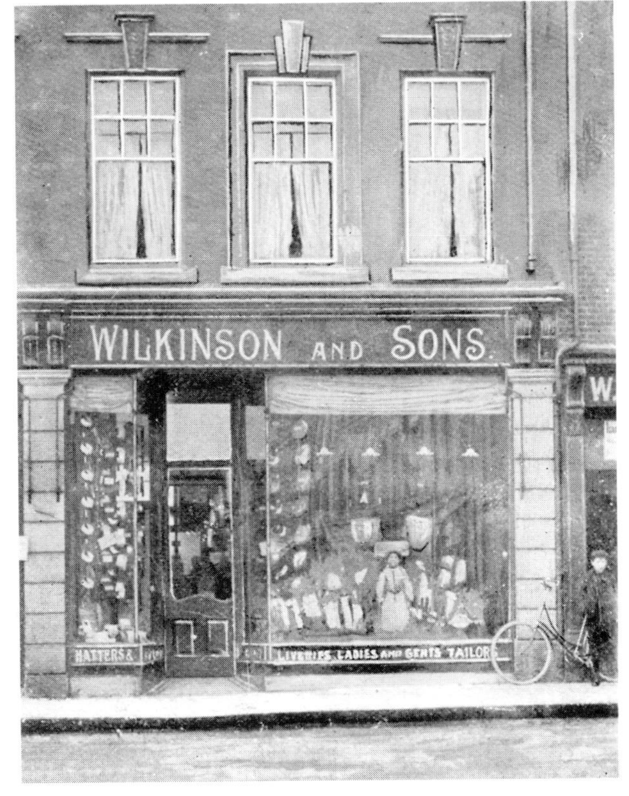

Right: At Market Place West was W.S. Wilkinson & Sons. They stated in 1907 that they were the leading house of gents' outfitting. The owners in later years sold ladies' clothes to add to the fierce competition in Morpeth for such goods.

Above: A relatively quiet scene up Newgate Street. This photograph formed the front of a postcard posted in Morpeth in 1904.

Left: If you were a wine drinker in 1907 Schofields Agricultural and Dispensing Chemists was the place to try a different blend. Glendinnings Beef & Malt Wine was said to be the best. Schofield also had their own brands of 'Magic Corn Plasters', 'Balsam Liquorice for Coughs' and 'Magic Drops for Lumbago'. Simm & Webb now have the premises at No 32.

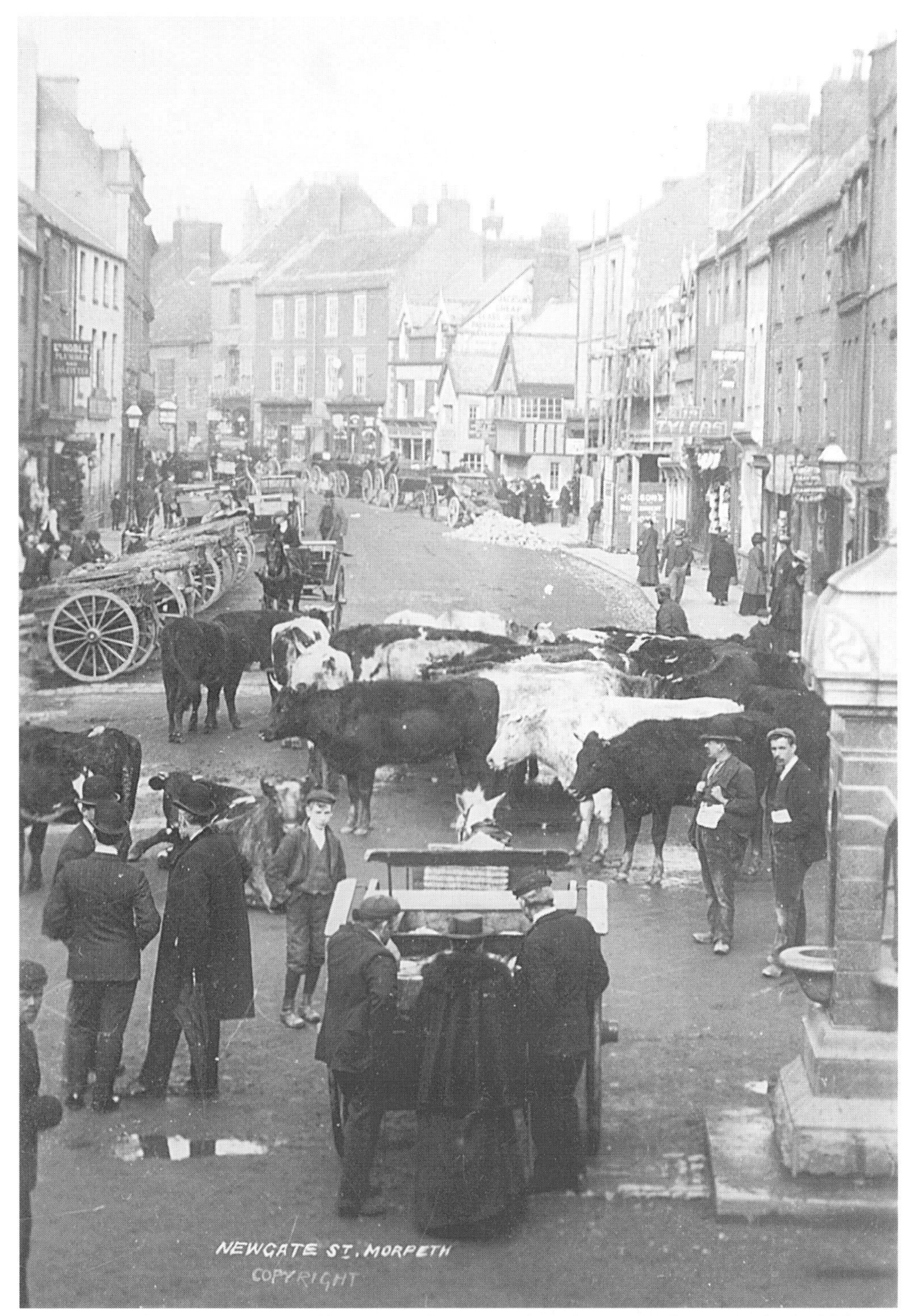

Newgate Street on market day around 1900. The chaos cattle caused could be imagined when up to a thousand head would cover the streets.

As well as producing lemonade, lime juice and ginger beer, George Young's Chantry Wells had long forgotten flavours to tempt customers – Potass Water, Seltza Water, Lithie Water, Hop Bitters and Kile Champagne. These were all made from water drawn from a deep artesian well on the premises.

Up Newgate Street to the Cottingwood Nurseries was E. Norman, a seedsman, nurseryman, florist and landscape gardener.

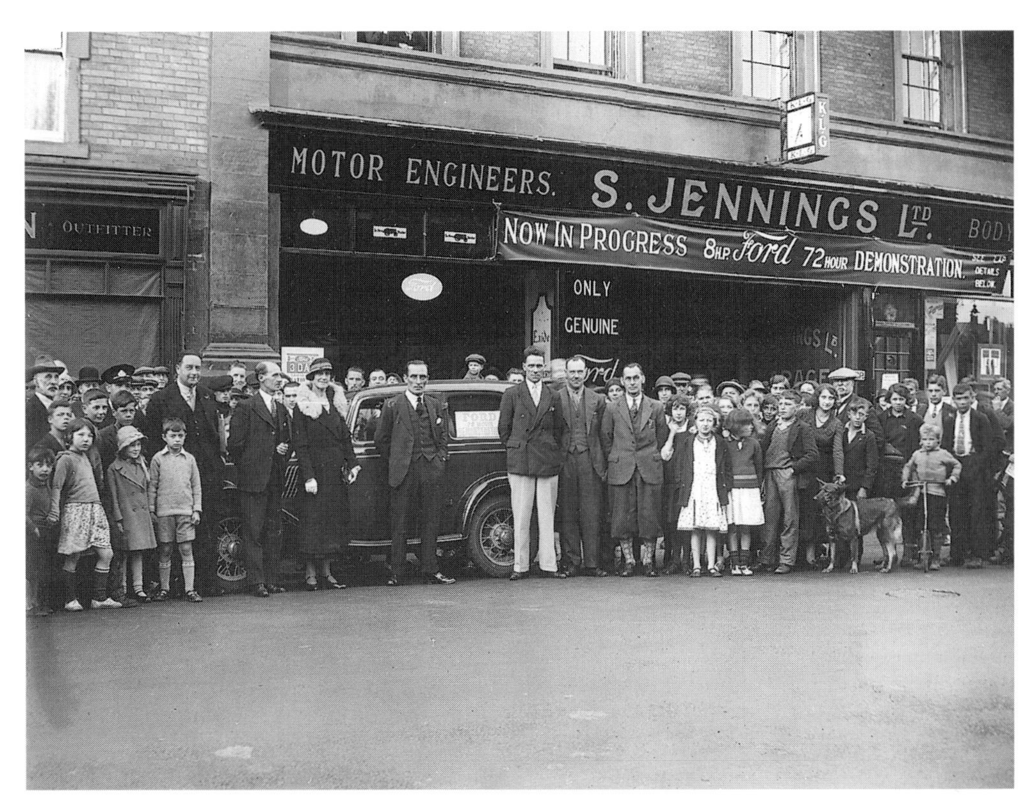

Above: A large crowd gathers in front of Jennings in Bridge Street in 1933. In its early years the firm was know mainly as bicycle specialists but now Jennings of Morpeth is a nationwide dealer for Ford cars.

Right: Thomas Matheson & Son were nurserymen in the town for over 300 years. The shop front down Oldgate bears two dates; 1689 being farther back in time. This 1943 catalogue does its best to encourage people to 'grow their own' in wartime.

R.T. & J. Hewitt steam Sentinal, ready to leave Shrewsbury for its journey up to Morpeth in July 1930. It was given the registration number TY 7501. Note the new pneumatic front wheels for a smoother ride. The bunker at the rear could carry $5^{1}/_{2}$ cwts of coal and the water tank had a capacity of 225 gallons.

A lot of heavy haulage companies started their business as timber hauliers. Hewitt's being no exception. The driver would have to be aware on corners as the load overhangs the rear bogie.

Hewitt early steam Sentinel fleet number 10, looking as though it has just arrived from Shrewsbury works. Note the chain drive to the rear wheels. This vehicle weighed in empty at seven ton 2 cwts.

In 1932 Hewitt moved the pedestrian bridge from Oldgate to Low Stanners. A Hewitt steam Sentinel (new to them in 1930) was the tractor unit and the bridge was conveyed on a pair of solid tyred twin bogies. As with most of these abnormal load moves it always drew in a lot of spectators. This would be a good local move for Hewitt as their depot was at North Garage, Spring Garden, Morpeth.

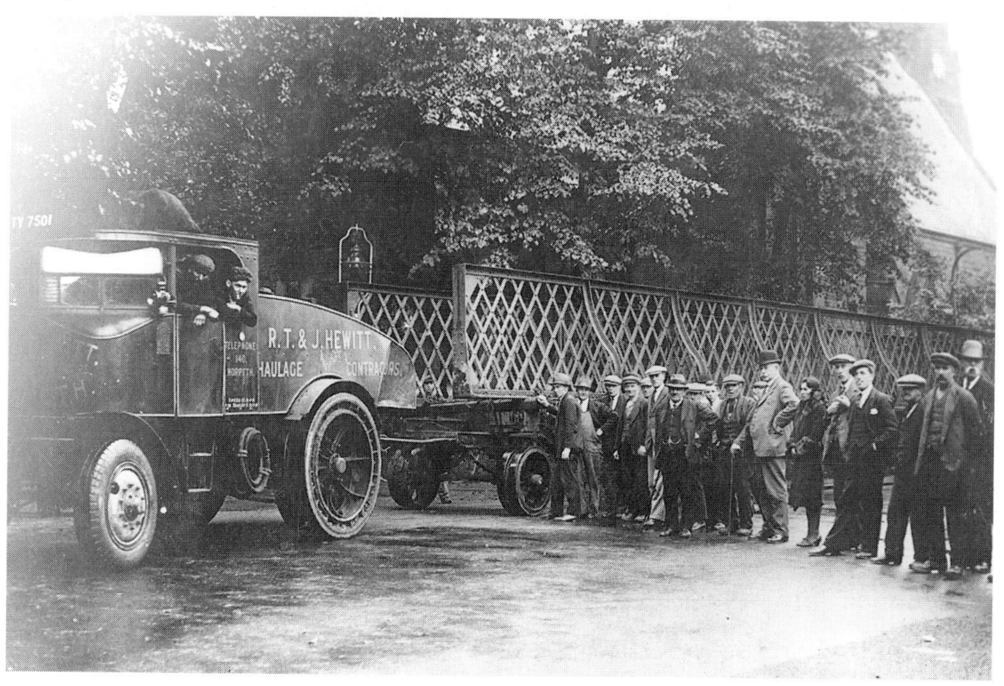

A general view of Swinney's engineering works in 1922, before the building of new offices. The site is now taken up by Safeways store.

Swinney's football team of 1959-60. Back row: B. Winship, J. Pratt, J. Hawkes, I. Spence, A. McLevy, R. Whitton, L. Brown, E. Weallans, J. Smith, J. Smith. Front row: A. McCurly, J. Jordan, R. Marley, L. Smith, N. Lamb. The mascot is also a Smith.

July 1930 Smith's Dock Journal

"SMITHS"
(SMITHS DOCK CO., LTD.)

OIL-BURNING INSTALLATIONS FOR LAND AND MARINE USE

PRESSURE, AIR AND STEAM JET SYSTEMS

CASTINGS
OF ALL DESCRIPTIONS
ROUGH OR MACHINED
FOR LAND OR MARINE WORK

GALLEY RANGES, COAL OR OIL FIRED

BRICK-MAKING MACHINERY

"SWINCAST" SPECIAL MIXTURE FOR CAST-IRON PIPELINES

Group of representative pipes and fittin to Admiralty specification and tests for New Singapore Dock (1928).

STEAM HEATED COOKING PANS

GROOVED PULLEYS OF ALL KINDS

GRINDING MILLS FOR CLAY, MORTAR, ETC.

STEAM-HEATED PRESSES FOR FOOD OR PLATES

MACHINE CAST WHEELS OF ALL KINDS

SMITH'S PATENT OIL BURNING INSTALLATIONS,

For estimates and full particulars apply to Sole Licensees & Manufacturers:

SWINNEY BROS. LTD., ENGINEERS & IRONFOUNDERS,

WANSBECK IRON WORKS, MORPETH, NORTHUMBERLAND

TELEGRAMS: "CIVOIL, MORPETH." TELEPHONE: 92 MORPETH (2 LINES)

i.

An advert for Swinney Brothers from 1930 showing their vast array of products. At this time they would supply numerous Northumberland collieries, brickworks, factories and hospitals. In later years they supplied international companies, such as Shell, for the off-shore oil industry.

After a hard day at work or shopping where better to be than the theatre for a night's entertainment and relaxation. Payne's Avenue Theatre had been the main place for silent movies and variety shows. The Coliseum opened to the public in December 1924. These photographs show its construction. The main contractor was Jonathan Wilson of No 25 Oldgate.

SPORTING MORPETH

Some Morpeth representatives at the East Northumberland Games were, standing: Duncan Dick, Alan Patterson and Jim Clark. Sitting: Lawrence Smith and Alan Morton. Morton was a good enough footballer to play for England Schoolboys at 15 years of age.

Football was always the game to play at Junior School level and the East Northumberland Schools leagues involving schools across Ashington, Morpeth and Bedlington areas were highly organised and successful.

The 1934 St James' School side won the East Northumberland League Cup. Back row: Mr Trainer, J. Waterson, Fred Varley, Alf Potts, Billy Cowgill, Ray Henderson, Mr Dodds. Front row: Eddie Moore, J. Proudlock, R. Lumley, J. Martin, Lewis Clark and Cecil Todd.

Twenty-three years later and Stobhillgate Junior School were doing well in the 'Little Schools' league. Fred Carruthers, the headteacher, had been a very competent footballer between the wars, playing wing half for both Bedlington United and Blyth Spartans. The younger teacher, Edwin Grieve, is well known in the Morpeth area as a first class speaker, writer and historian. The boys are, back row: Eric Brady, David Mitcheson, Ron Appleby, Keith Soulsby, Michael Johnstone, Billy Jamieson, Frank Ord, Michael Allon, Richard Tinlin. Front row: Gordon Rice, Peter Wilson, Billy Roberts, George Lowther and Michael Hunter.

Carrying on to Senior School level and provided you didn't go to the Grammar School, up Cottingwood, you continued with your soccer. This senior football team was from Newminster Modern and coached by John Wharrier in 1959.

As with most sports, schoolchildren are first encouraged to excel at home and school. Judging by the enthusiasm of this Mitford Road School group in 1948, athletics was a favourite. Sports Day fanatics include: Bill Ricalton, Gordon Prior (Hank the Yank), Bobby Whitton, Brian Routledge, Sonny Macauley, Margaret Hepple, Isobel Price and Irene Watson.

Like every other town in the North East, Morpeth had many football clubs. Morpeth Town FC was which was run by Bill Craik for many years, then later his son, Ralphie, took over in the 1960s. The club is now in the Albany Northern League, under the guidance of local lad Ken Beattie, and are now based at Craik Park. There were also teams at both Northgate and St George's Hospitals, which played in the now defunct Coquetdale League, joining such teams as Longhirst, Pegswood, Morpeth Black Watch and Morpeth Villa.

An example of the statue of Morpeth based clubs is the remarkable saga of the Northumberland FA Senior Cup in 1886. 'Morpeth' fought their way to the semi-finals where they were paired with Shankhouse. After drawn games at home and away, and another three replays, it was still stalemate. With penalty shoot-outs and 'golden goals' still a century away, the clubs, with the blessing of the Northumberland FA, agreed to toss a coin with whoever winning taking their place in the final. The proviso was that if that team won the final, the two clubs would share the trophy for six months each. Shankhouse won the toss and went onto beat Newcastle West End (later to become Newcastle United) in the final. So Morpeth have the rare honour of having 'won' the Senior Cup without playing in the final. Seven years later, in 1903, Morpeth Harriers won the Senior Cup to become only the second Morpeth-based winners. In the other County competition, Morpeth Town have triumphed in 1979 and 1986.

In 1962/63 an unofficial league began playing, and on 13th August 1963 a meeting was held in the Black & Grey in Copper Chare with the view to starting an official league. The Morpeth Sunday friendly league came into existence with eleven clubs taking part, including four from Morpeth: Blue Rangers, Fire Brigade, St Robert's and Morpeth Co-op. This league has now expanded to four divisions with over 40 clubs from the north and east of the county. The secretary elected at that meeting, Syd Johnson, is still in that post after 42 years. Syd is also Vice-President of Northumberland FA. Two other football 'notables' in Morpeth were Stan Seymour Jnr, President of Northumberland FA and Jim McKay, Secretary of the Northern Alliance for many years.

Blue Rangers, Morpeth Sunday League team, 1965. Back row: J. Johnson, W. Swann, A. Thornton, T. Luckey, N. Fraser, T. Kelly, J. Halliday, J. Kidd. Front row: Syd Johnson, F. Brady, R. Dobson, H. Gebbie and J.W. Kidd.

It's Twickenham or bust for Morpeth!

Morpeth Rugby Club's biggest game was on Saturday, 5th April 1975 when the club's senior side took on the mighty Rosslyn Park in the RFU National Knock-out Competition semi-final. Victory meant an appearance at Twickenham in the final against either Bedford or Coventry. Brian Keenlyside was Morpeth's star man and kicker. He scored in the game but the minnows of Morpeth were out-classed on the day losing 28-6 to the Andy Ripley (England) led Londoners. Morpeth's team on the day was: B. Keenleyside, K. Fraser, W. Casey, A. McMillan, R. Thornton, W. Howitt, I. Blakey, M. Storey, I. May, J Dixon, B. Garnett, C. Ferguson, D. Learmouth, I. Pringle and D. Pringle.

Not to be outdone, Morpeth's Second 15, 'The Reivers' won the Northumberland RFM Senior Cup for Second 15s in April 1969. Heroes of the hour – Back row: Michael Clark, Jeff Robinson, Alex Park, Harry Kennedy, Dick McHenry, Fraser Hunter, Bob Young, Jim Wakenshaw. Front row: Hamish McGeoch, Gordon Wilkinson, Peter Givens, Harry Little, Bernard Scott (captain), Stuart Inchmore and John Candy.

Cricket has been played in and around Morpeth for many years. Most people will remember Stobhill as the cricket field but Morpeth sides turned out at High Stanners in the 1860s later moving to what is now the Mitford Road Rugby Ground. Morpeth Cricket Club was a founder member of the Tyneside Senior League in 1904, moving to the Alnwick & District League where the championship was won in 1922. Few older cricket pictures are there, than this of the Morpeth Grammar School side of 1862. Back row: Lea, Sewell, Jobling, Henderson, Cocks, Younger. Front row: A. Purdy, Harrison, Swan, Maclaran and B. Purdy.

Sharing its home with the Cricket Club is the Men's Hockey Club. It is said many cricketers played hockey as their winter game hence the field sharing. Origins can be traced back to the 1920s when the field was shared, on Pegswood Moor, with Morpeth Ladies' Hockey Club. The picture, taken on Stobhill Field, was of the hockey men in the mid 1950s.

Athletics in Morpeth has always been popular. In modern times the Morpeth to Newcastle half marathon has attracted 'fun runners' on a New Year's Day. This 1932 photograph seems to emphasise the importance of the race to club and international athletes who would be supported all the way along the route to Newcastle.

A Morpeth Harriers Club group of the late 1940s.

International athlete Brendan Foster maintains Jim Alder was a pioneer for athletics in the North East. Jim was totally dedicated to the sport and among his achievements were the Commonwealth Marathon title in Jamaica's heat in 1966 and the 30km world record set in 1970. After his 'retirement' Jim spent much of his spare time encouraging youngsters.

In 1982 he published his biography *Marathon And Chips* by Arthur McKenzie, a former Newcastle policeman and writer of television programmes such as *The Bill* and *Casualty*. Arthur was a discus thrower who also competed in the Commonwealth Games.

Chief Inspector, Ernest D. Surtees, who lived in Alexander Road in his later years, went around the world in sailing ships when only in his early teens. During the First World War, he became an officer and served in the ill-fated Northumberland Hussars at the Battle of the Somme. He was gassed and wounded but after convalescence in England, became a pilot in the Royal Flying Corps.

After the war, as a member of Surrey Athletic Club, he because one of the first sprinters to record 10 seconds for the 100 yards, beating the Champions of Australia and New Zealand. He later became Police National Champion at 100 yards and 220 yards.

A major professional sporting event took place between 1874-1958. Around 1890 it became known as the 'Morpeth Olympic Games' and attracted runners from all over the world. The main event was the 110 yards sprint. However, there were other events such as the 80 yards, 220 yards, half mile, pole vault and wrestling.

Several venues were used during its history, ending up at the Grange House Field. During the 20th century only two Morpeth runners won the big sprint, Matt Graham and Raymond Surtees (running under the name of R. Anderson) who recorded the fastest ever time in 1948 when only 18 years of age (*right*).

Below: Raymond Surtees winning the 1948 110 yards handicap.

Morpeth Olympic Games drew the best athletes in the North of England, the Borders and even way into Scotland, all seeking the title of Olympic Champion. The meeting, held on August Bank Holiday Saturday and Monday, was in its heyday just after the Second World War. Many sporting activities were to be seen in the natural amphitheatre on the Mitford Road, just past Morpeth Rugby Club. As well as sprinting 80 yards and 110 yards, there was also middle distance events, all handicapped with the best runners off scratch. While the races were in progress, there was the added attraction of the high jump with a little bit of Cumberland and Westmorland wrestling thrown in for good measure. Some of the best athletes took part in every event, such as farmers George Davidson and his brother from Thorneyhaugh. George won the high jump title almost every year and one year won the sprint event, too.

Copper Reed and Neville Black of Ashington fight out the finish in a sprint at the Morpeth Olympics in 1951.

Nobbie Poxton (running as F. Loss), centre, wins the half mile in 1949.

The year 1950 was special as a real Olympian took part in the 110 yards sprint. American Barney Ewell (*right*) had been the favourite to win the sprint title at Wembley Stadium in 1948 in the first post-war Olympic Games, but lack of a photo-finish camera robbed the super-fast American of first place. In a fit of pique, Ewell turned professional and ran on the summer pro-circuit for a number of years.

OFFICIAL PROGRAMME, 6d.
1950.
SATURDAY, AUGUST 5th.

(69th MEETING).

MORPETH OLYMPIC GAMES

in OLD GRANGE HOUSE FIELD, MITFORD ROAD.

President: JOHN DUNN, Esq.

Vice - Presidents: Ald. W. S. SANDERSON, Ald. R. ELLIOTT, Messrs. J. R. TEMPLE, J. T. CHARLTON, H. P. CHARLTON, A. ARROWSMITH, JOHN GRAY, A. W. L. DAVY and S. RUTHERFORD.

Committee: Ald. W. S. SANDERSON, Ald. R. ELLIOTT, Messrs H. P. CHARLTON, J. T. CHARLTON, W. WRIGHT, JAS. NICHOLSON, JOHN B. NICHOLSON, FRED. RUTHERFORD, STANLEY RUTHERFORD, N. WYLIE, A. ARROWSMITH, JOHN WRIGHT, JOHN ELLIOTT, JAS. ED. NICHOLSON, and R. ARROWSMITH.

Secretary: Mr. JAMES NICHOLSON, 2, St. Mary's Field, Morpeth.
Treasurer: Mr. A. W. L. DAVY.
Handicappers: Messrs. T. and D. BLACKBURN, Newsham, Blyth.
Starter: Mr. J. MILGATE, Blyth.
Marksmen: Messrs JACK and JAMES BROWN.

1. **£40 Half - Mile HANDICAP.** 1st, £30; 2nd, £7; £3 divided amongst other Finalists.
2. **£130 110 YARDS FOOT HANDICAP** (HEATS ONLY).
3. **£20 220 YARDS FOOT HANDICAP** (Non - Penalty). 1st, £10; 2nd, £5. £5 amongst other Finalists.
4. **£45 WRESTLING** (Cumberland and Westmorland Style).
   £15 10½ Stones. 1st, £7 10/-; 2nd, £3; 3rd, 30/-. Falls 2/6.
   £15 for 12 Stones. Same Prizes.
   £15 for ALL WEIGHTS. Same Prizes.
5. **£20 POLE VAULT.** 1st Prize, £10; 2nd, £4; 3rd, £3; 4th and 5th, 30/- each. There must be at least two bona-fide competitors for this event, and to qualify for prize-money 9ft. must be cleared.
6. **£5 RUNNING HIGH LEAP.** 1st Prize, 70/-; 2nd, 20/-; 3rd, 10/-.
7. **QUOITS HANDICAP** (On the Sward). 70/- added to Entries.

The Games Committee reserve the power to make such alterations in the programme as they think necessary, including the power to adjust or reduce the cash prizes, or to postpone the sports wholly or partly to a future day in the event of storm. The decision of the Committee will in every case be final.

ADMISSION TO FIELD EACH DAY: ADULTS 2/6, CHILDREN 1/-.

Bookmakers' Stands 12/6 each day (includes Number Men). **Cars 5/-.**

Crandstand 2/6. **Ring Seats 1/-.**
SATURDAY: GATES OPEN 1 P.M. COMMENCE 2-15 P.M.
MONDAY: GATES OPEN 12 O'clock. COMMENCE 1 P.M.

Refreshments:
Luncheons, Teas and Light Refreshments by Mr. DAVID C. ABSALOM.

Liquor Tent:
R. EDGAR & CO., Morpeth.

J. & J. S. MACKAY, MORPETH.

The front cover of the programme for the 69th Morpeth Olympic Games, Saturday 5th August 1950. For the £130 110 yards handicap there were 28 heats with nine runners in each race – 252 athletes in total! Barney Ewell was in heat 25 and was the only man running off scratch. In heat 24 was sixteen-year-old M. Kirkup of Ashington. Mike Kirkup later became a well-known historian and author.

Faced with strong competition from television and a lack of interest from younger athletes, professional running waned, and the Morpeth Olympics were discontinued in 1958.

Some of the town's businessmen are pictured here as successful members of Morpeth Bowling Club, winners of two cups in 1930 and 1931. Back row: T.S. Fawcett, F. Rowe, J. Allan, R. Tully, G. Sawyers, F. Cooper, J. Wilson. Middle row: C. Lloyd, W. Allan, T. Swinney, J.J. James, E. Lamb, J. Laidler. Front row: R. Parkin, C.P. Roll, W. Bowman and J. Baston.

Morpeth Golf Club was formed at a meeting held at the Queen's Head on 23rd April 1906. Dr Phillips was the first chairman and the first clubhouse was the Sun Inn. This gathering of founder members includes Doctors Dickie and Phillips.

SOME NEARBY VILLAGES

All small stations employed plenty of staff and this postcard from around 1906 shows the Stannington Station Master on the right and some of the other workers. Stannington Station, on the main East Coast Line, was closed to passenger services on 15th September 1958 and goods traffic on 10th August 1964.

Stannington

Another view of Stannington Station at the turn of the last century.

Cycling was not a cheap form of transport in 1908 (date of this photograph) as bicycles could cost into double figures if bought new. Stannington's annual Summer Church Parade for cyclists drew enthusiasts from all over the area.

Like many Northumberland villages, Stannington had its school and some children would walk quite a distance to attend daily. Up until the early days after the Second World War many village schools, some Church of England, had only one teacher, with pupil teachers as helpers. Many headteachers of Northumberland village schools stayed for their whole careers in the same place. It was not unknown for a village school to have only three heads over a century.

Moving on to 1913 and Stannington School's fancy dress parade brought out Kaiser Bill (front) a year ahead of his time.

These two postcards of the centre of Stannington have date stamps of 1911. Stannington is regarded in 2003 as a nice place to live with recent house building doing nothing to take away the friendly village atmosphere it has always had. An active Women's Institute group, History Society, Church and popular pub go a long way to help villages gel.

For many villages, the Church of England was the centre of local life. The building obviously symbolising the place to worship but also during the week was a meeting place for villagers. This photograph dates from around 1910.

Stannington village, *circa* 1920. The car parked on the right belongs to Mr Johnston, the postcard photographer from Gateshead. The number '2008' after Stannington is his reference number for his Monarch Series of postcards. He took over 16,000 different North East views in this series.

Stannington Children's TB Sanatorium, established in 1907, was the first purpose-built hospital of its kind in Britain. Children stayed for months, sometimes years, but not everyone enjoyed the experience.

Right: Jack Dunsmore at the sanatorium in 1926 with his mother and father. Jack recalls: 'I was diagnosed with TB glands of the bowel and was admitted to Stannington Sanatorium in the Brough baby ward, where I was a patient for one year. It was one of the unhappiest periods of my young life. I detested it. Parents were only allowed to visit once a month for two hours. No other visitor was allowed and it was very traumatic for the child. The ward sister was cruel and vindictive. She appeared to have a dislike for me and she hit me for no reason, locked me in the bathroom and made me eat fat meat, which I threw out of the window, when her back was turned. Prior to the visit of parents, you were warned not to complain and of the consequences if you did. I still have vivid memories of Stannington Sanatorium and how much I and others hated the place.'

Below: A souvenir postcard produced to commemorate the visit to the Sanatorium by the Duke of York, 28th May 1926.

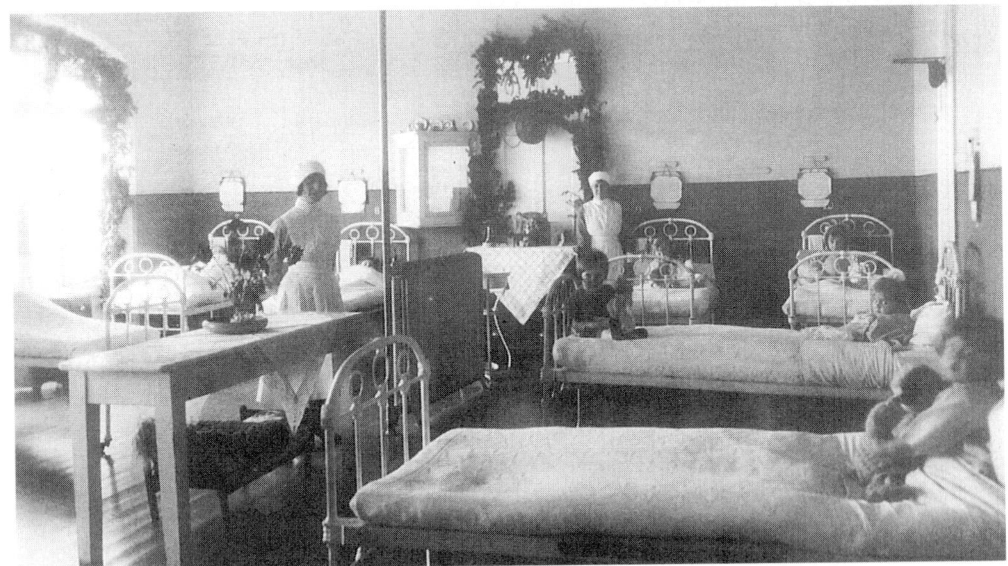

Above and below: The Vita Glass Pavillion, Stannington Sanatorium. Note the open windows to provide the children with lots of fresh air.

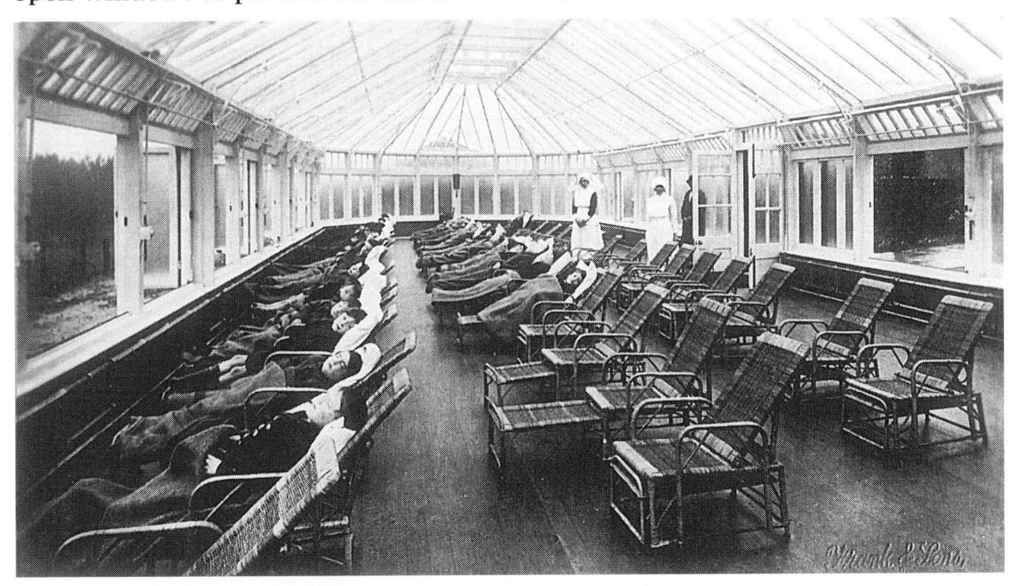

The nurses home at Stannington.

Longhorsley

Longhorsley in 1924. A view of Coronation Terrace, looking towards the crossroads. The Comrades hut can be seen behind the blacksmith's shop.

A time for the Longhorsley ladies and girls to get out their best hats for the annual choir trip in 1911.

Village life in rural Northumberland often centred around the school and church. Children would be told, in advance, of the photographer's visit. Best shirts, jumpers, shoes and dresses came out on the big day, although fashions didn't seem to have changed much in the 13 years between these Longhorsley School groups (1910 & 1923).

Longhorsley School, *circa* 1923. Front row: third left, Wilf Monaghan; second right, Jack Green. Middle row, left to right: Jimmy Green, Dora Green, Isa Lennox, Olga Lennox, Renee Lennox, Alison Carr, Ada Monaghan, Jean Monaghan, Joe Sheerin. Back row: far left, Bob Monaghan; third right, Larry Sheerin; second, Peter Carr.

Mitford

Mitford Village main street, *circa* 1930.

The name seems to have remained unchanged for centuries (unlike many other villages) and perhaps the name was devised from its position near the fords of Font and Wansbeck.

In the past, Mitford had a flourishing market but when Morpeth was granted, in 1199, the privilege of having a market, Mitford suffered and bitter jealousies arose between the two places with Mitford folk taunting Morpethians with the couplet:

Mitford was Mitford when Morpeth was Nyen
And Mitford will be Mitford when Morpeth is Gyen.

Mitford Church and Vicarage. The Old Vicarage built in the 1770s housed the family of probably the village's most famous vicar, Rev R.C. Macleod (1897-1937) who took hundreds of photographs of Mitford and its surrounds, many of which are stored at the County Record Office. This building was replaced by the new vicarage in 1973.

Mitford Hall, from a postcard sent in 1911. John Dobson designed this building and work started on it in 1812, being completed in 1828.

William Bertram held Mitford during the reign of Henry I and in 1135 he started building the Church and Castle. Two hundred years later the Castle was destroyed after being attacked. The building was dismantled and the stones were used for the building of walls, houses, etc.

A peaceful village scene in Mitford. The Pipe Rolls of 1196 give the village the title 'Midford', but Mitford is the name generally used over the centuries.

Mitford Manor House was built next to the Church for the Mitford family. The porch tower bears the coat of arms of Robert Mitford and the date 1637.

Two lovely postcard views of rural life in Mitford. *Above*: Well dressed ladies and girls pose for the photographer near the bridge in the early years of the 20th century. *Below*: A later view of men at work at the village smithy.

Hepscott

Hepscott village blacksmith, Tom Cowans, at his shop, *circa* 1905.

North Eastern Railway's Hepscott Station on the old Blyth & Tyne branch, from a postcard dated 1906. The station opened in 1858 and closed to passenger services on 3rd April 1950.

Two views from the burn in Hepscott, taken from almost the same spot but years apart. Brook Cottage and Brookside are in the background.

The Oak Inn is built on a pond that was previously filled in. Formerly an ash tree stood at the south east corner of the inn and when the builders removed it they thought it an oak, from which the inn gets its name. There is reputed to be a hoard of coins buried near another ash tree at Causey Park and is known as the 'hidden hoard of Causey'. There is also the tale of the phantom horses of Causey Park. Whenever they appear they are said to pasage a death in the area. The last reported sighting of 'the steeds' was in 1911 when they frightened a herd of cattle which were found lying down, terrified, at Acklington Road Ends, two and a half miles away. The phantom horses (a pair of greys) always gallop along an old Roman road which runs through the estate, heading towards the south east.

Three superb motors at Espley Hall, one time residence of George Bainbridge and in later years a hostelry of quality, with nine bedrooms.

THE PEOPLE'S HISTORY

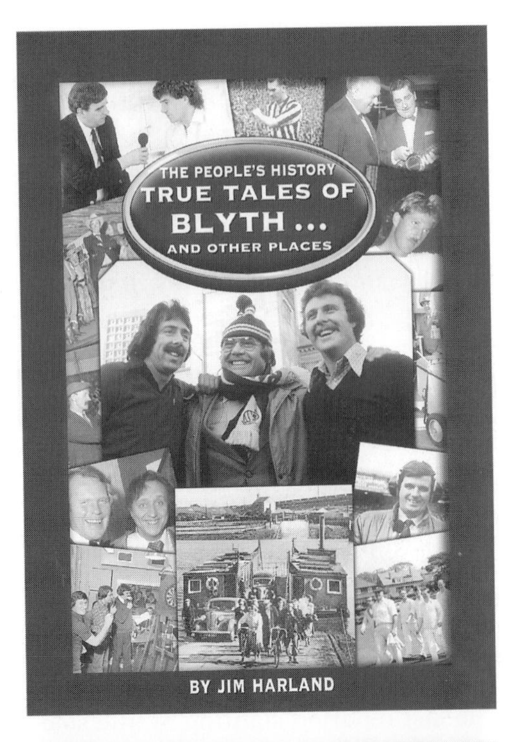

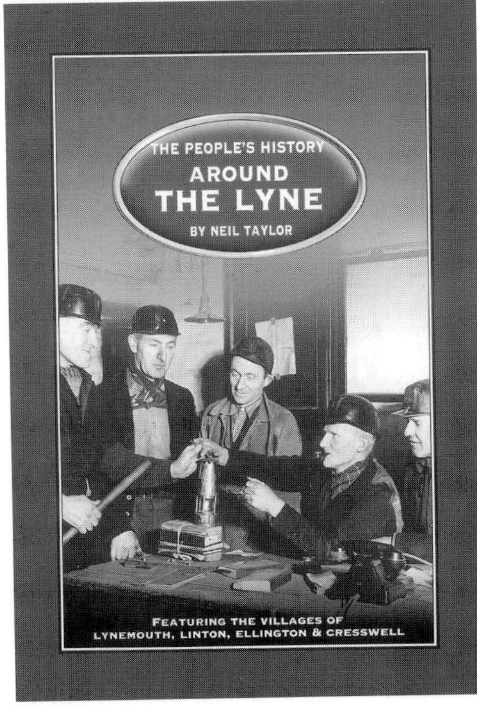

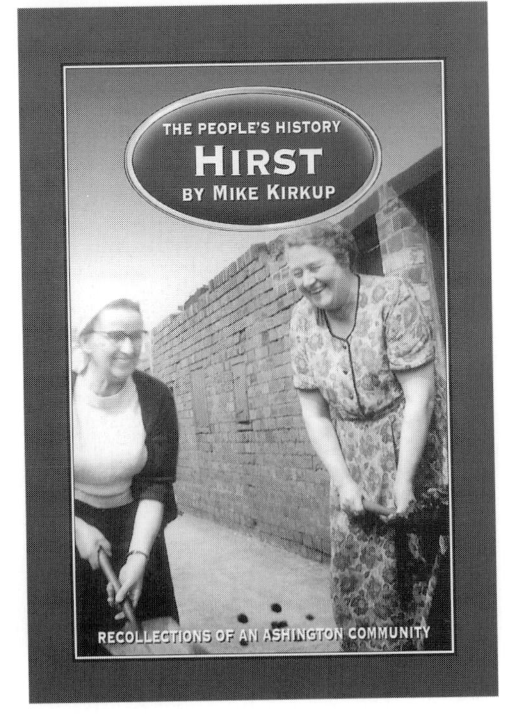

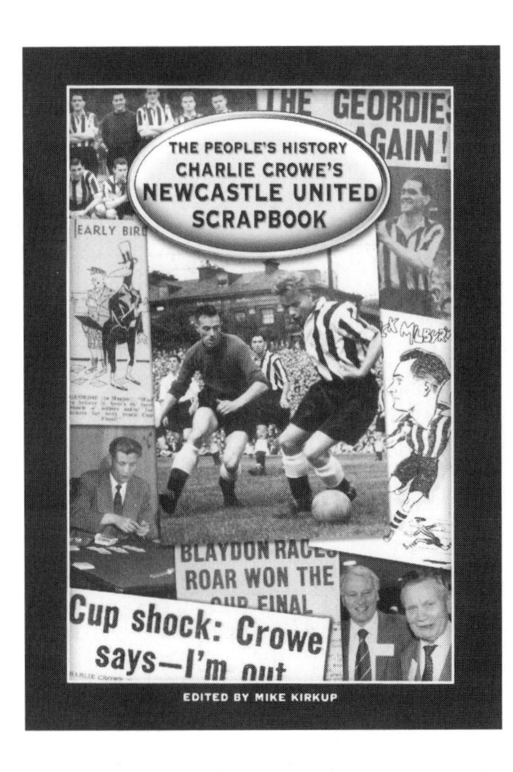
THE GEORDIES AGAIN!
THE PEOPLE'S HISTORY
CHARLIE CROWE'S
NEWCASTLE UNITED
SCRAPBOOK
EARLY BIRD
BLAYDON RACES
ROAR WON THE
Cup shock: Crowe
says—I'm out
EDITED BY MIKE KIRKUP

THE PEOPLE'S HISTORY
COP
ON THE TYNE
BY ARTHUR MCKENZIE

THE PEOPLE'S HISTORY
GEORDIE MUDDLING
BY RIPYARD
CUDDLING
A COLLECTION OF GEORDIE POETRY
BY JACK DAVITT

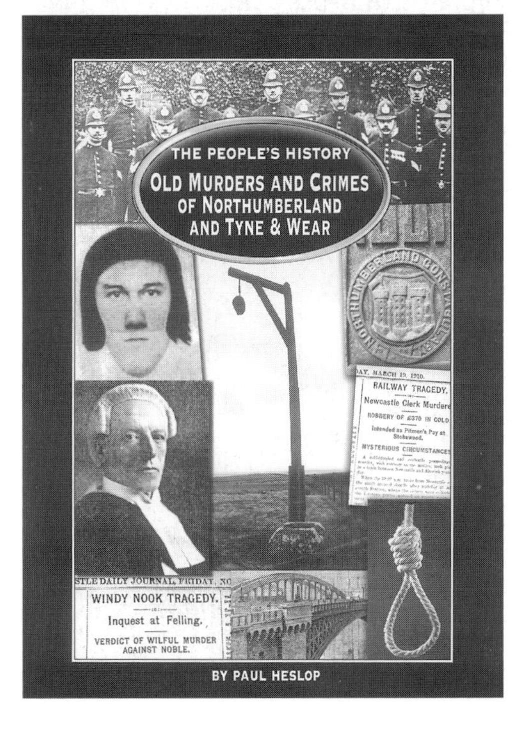
THE PEOPLE'S HISTORY
OLD MURDERS AND CRIMES
OF NORTHUMBERLAND
AND TYNE & WEAR
RAILWAY TRAGEDY.
Newcastle Clerk Murdered
WINDY NOOK TRAGEDY.
Inquest at Felling.
VERDICT OF WILFUL MURDER
AGAINST NOBLE.
BY PAUL HESLOP

Children pose on the Stepping Stones. A postcard sent in 1911.

The People's History

To receive a catalogue of our latest titles send a large SAE to:

The People's History
Suite 1
Byron House
Seaham Grange Business Park
Seaham
County Durham
SR7 0PY